KETO DIET

POWER PRESSURE COOKER XL COOKBOOK

Easy Low-Carb, Weight Loss Recipes For Your Power Pressure Cooker XL

Brenda Coon

ISBN: 978-1983850288

Warning-Disclaimer

The purpose of this book is to educate and entertain. The author or publisher does not guarantee that anyone following the techniques, suggestions, tInstant Pots, ideas, or strategies will become successful. The author and publisher shall have neither liability or responsibility to anyone with respect to any loss or damage caused, or alleged to be caused, directly or indirectly by the information contained in this book.

Contents

Introduction

Want to follow a ketogenic diet but not sure where to start? Struggling with finding delicious and tummy-filling recipes when going "against the grains"? Do not worry! This book will not only provide you with amazing keto recipes that will get you started in a jiffy, but it will also teach you the ultimate tricks for adopting a keto lifestyle forever.

Mouth-watering delights for any occasion and for any type of eater, you will not believe that these recipes will help you restore your health and slim your body. Ditching carbs does not mean ditching yummy treats, and with these ingenious recipes, you will see that for yourself.

Successfully practiced for more than nine decades, the ketogenic diet has proven to be the ultimate long-term diet for any person. The restriction list may frighten many, but the truth is, this diet is super adaptable, and the food combinations and tasty meals are endless.

Try these delicacies and see what I am talking about.

Ketogenic Diet – The New Lifestyle

It is common knowledge that our bodies are designed to run on carbohydrates. We use them to provide our bodies with the energy required for normal functioning. However, what many people are clueless about is that carbs are not the only source of fuel our bodies can use. Just like they can run on carbs, our bodies can also use fats as an energy source. When we ditch the carbs and focus on providing our bodies with more fat, we are embarking on the ketogenic train.

Despite what many people think, the ketogenic diet is not just another fad diet. It has been around since 1920 and has resulted in outstanding results and amazingly successful stories. If you are new to the keto world and have no idea what I am talking about, let me simplify this for you.

In order for you to truly understand what the ketogenic diet is all about and why you should choose to follow it, let me first explain what happens to your body after consuming a carb-loaded meal.

Imagine you have just swallowed a giant bowl of spaghetti. Your tummy is full, your taste buds are satisfied, and your body is provided with more carbs than necessary. After consumption, your body immediately starts the process of digestion, during which your body will break down the consumed carbs into glucose, which is a source of energy your body depends on. So one might ask, "What is wrong with carbs?" Actually, there are a number of things. For starters, they raise the blood sugar, they make us fat, and in short, they hurt our overall health.

So, how can a ketogenic diet help?

A ketogenic diet skips this process by lowering the carbohydrate intake and providing high fat and moderate protein levels. Now, since there is no adequate amount of carbs to use as energy, your liver is forced to find the fuel elsewhere. And since your body is packed with lots of fat, the liver starts using these extra levels of fat as an energy source.

THE KETOSIS

Once your liver begins preparing your body for the fuel change, the fat from the liver will start producing ketones – hence the name KETOgenic. What glucose is for the carbs, the ketones are for the fat, meaning they are the tiny molecules created once the fat is broken down to be used as energy.

The switch from glucose to ketones is something that has pushed many people away from this diet. There are people who consider this to be a dangerous process, but the truth is, your body will run just as efficiently on ketones as it does on glucose.

Once your body shifts to using ketones as fuel, you are in the state of *ketosis*. Ketosis is a metabolic process that may be interpreted as a little 'shock' to your body. However, this is far from dangerous. Every change in life requires adaptation, and so does this.

This adaptation process is really not set in stone, and every person goes through ketosis differently. However, for most people it takes around two weeks to fully adapt to the new lifestyle.

Just remember, this is all biological and completely normal. You have spent your whole life packing your body with glucose; it is only natural that you need time to adapt to the new dietary change.

THE BENEFITS OF KETO DIET

Even though it is still considered 'controversial', the ketogenic diet is actually the best dietary choice one can make. From weight loss to longevity, here are the benefits that following a ketogenic diet can bring to your life:

Loss of Appetite

Cannot tame your cravings? Do not worry. This diet will neither leave you exhausted nor with a rumbling gut. The ketogenic diet will actually help you say no to that second piece of cake. Once you train your body to run on fat and not on carbs, you will experience a drop in your appetite that will work magic for your figure.

Weight Loss

Since the body is forced to produce only a small amount of glucose, it will also be forced to lower the insulin productivity. When that happens, your kidneys will start getting rid of the extra sodium, which will lead to weight loss.

HDL Cholesterol Increase

While consuming a diet high in fat and staying clear of the harmful glucose, your body will experience a rise in the good HDL cholesterol levels, which will in turn reduce the risk for many cardiovascular problems.

Drop in Blood Pressure

Cutting back on carbs will also drop your blood pressure. The drop in the blood pressure can prevent many health problems such as strokes or heart diseases.

Lower Risk of Diabetes

Although this probably goes without saying, it is important to mention this one. When you ditch the carbs, your body is forced to lower the glucose productivity significantly, which obviously leads to a lower risk of diabetes.

Improved Brain Function

Many studies have shown that replacing carbohydrates with fat as an energy source leads to mental clarity and improved brain function. This is yet another reason why you should go keto.

Longevity

I am not saying this diet will turn you into a 120-hundred-year-old monk. However, it has been scientifically proven that once the oxidative stress levels are lowered, the lifespan is extended. And since this diet can result in a significant drop in the oxidative stress levels, the corresponding effect it could have on a person's lifespan is clear.

THE KETO PLATE

First of all, just because it is called a 'diet' does not mean you are about to spend your days in starvation. The ketogenic diet will neither tell you not to eat five times a day if you want to, nor will it leave your belly empty.

The only rule the keto diet has is to eat fewer carbohydrates, more foods that are high in fat, and consume a moderate protein intake. But how much is too much and what is the right amount? The general rule of a thumb is that your daily nutrition should consist of:

65-70 % fat

25-30 % protein

5 % carbohydrates

Or, to be more precise, it is not recommended that you consume more than twenty grams of carbs when on a ketogenic diet.

This macronutrient percentage, however, can be achieved in whichever way you and your belly are comfortable with. For instance, if you crave a carb meal now and want to eat, for instance, sixteen grams of carbs at once, you can do so as long as your other meals do not contain more than four grams of carbs combined.

Some of the recipes in this book offer zero grams of carbs, while others have a few grams. By making a proper meal plan that works for you, you can easily skip the inconvenience cloaked around this diet and start receiving the amazing benefits.

WHAT TO AVOID

In order to stay on track with your Keto diet, there are certain foods you need to say farewell to. Go to your kitchen and get rid of these tempting but super unhealthy ingredients:

- Sugar
- Diet Soda
- Starchy Vegetables. Potatoes, beans, parsnips, legumes, peas, and corn are usually packed with tons of carbs, so they should be avoided. However, sneaking some starch when your daily carb limit allows is not a sin.
- Grains. Rice, wheat, and everything made from grains such as pasta or bread are not allowed.
- Trans fats
- Refined Oils and Fats (corn oil, canola oil, etc)

WHAT TO EAT

Obviously, you can eat anything besides what is mentioned above; however, there are certain foods that will help you up your fat intake and provide you with more longer-lasting energy:

- Meat
- Whole Eggs
- Fish and Seafood
- Bacon
- Sausage
- Avocados
- Leafy Greens

- Non-Starchy Vegetables: Cucumber, Zucchini, Asparagus, Broccoli, Onion, Brussel Sprouts, Cabbage, Tomatoes, Eggplant, Sea Weed, Peppers, Squash
- Full-Fat Dairy (heavy cream, yogurt, sour cream, cheese, etc.)
- Nuts. Nuts are packed with healthy fats, but be careful when consuming pistachios, chestnuts, and cashews, as they contain more carbs than the rest of the nuts. Macadamia nuts, pecans, and almonds are the best for the Keto diet.
- Seeds

KETO SWAPS

Just because you are not allowed to eat rice or pasta doesn't mean you have to sacrifice eating risotto or spaghetti. Well, sort of. For every forbidden item on the keto diet there is a healthier replacement that will not contradict your dietary goal and will still taste amazing.

Here are the ultimate keto swaps you need to know in order to overcome the cravings quicker and become a Keto chef:

Bread and Buns - Bread made from nut flour, mushroom caps, cucumber slices

Wraps and tortillas - Wraps and tortillas made from nut flour, lettuce leaves, kale leaves

Pasta and spaghetti - Spiralized veggies such as zoodles, spaghetti squash, etc.

Lasagna Noodles - Zucchini or eggplant slices

Rice - Cauliflower rice (ground in a food processor)

Mashed potatoes - Mashed cauliflower or other veggies

Hash browns - Cauliflower or spaghetti squash

Flour - Coconut flour, nut flour

Bread crumbs - Almond flour

Pizza crust - Crust made with allowed flour, cauliflower crust

French fries - Carrot sticks, turnip fries, zucchini fries

Potato chips - Zucchini chips, kale chips

Croutons - Bacon bits, nuts, sunflower seeds, flax crackers

Power Pressure Cooker XL - Revolutionary Appliance

Pressure cookers offer an efficient, time-saving, and absolutely effortless way to enjoy a delicious meal without sacrificing the wonderful taste. But what was every housewife's favorite kitchen appliance in the 1950s has surely evolved into a powerful and much more convenient tool that every kitchen should be equipped with.

Electric pressure cookers may have been around since 1991, but it wasn't until recently that they really reached their peak. There are a couple of electric pressure cookers currently on the market – all with smart programming and the most satisfying options – however, there is one pressure cooker in particular that stands out and casts a shadow on its other competitors. The best electric pressure cooker you can currently buy is beyond doubt the Power Pressure Cooker XL.

Whether you already own one and are looking for some yummy recipes for your Power Pressure Cooker, or you need a little nudge that will convince you to buy one, one thing is certain: buying this book was definitely the smartest move.

Inside this book you will not only find over a hundred decadent and absolutely irresistible recipes (all with nutritional info) that satisfy everyone, but you will also learn what makes the Power Pressure Cooker XL so powerful and why it is worth the money you'll spend.

It may cook with pressure, but the Power Pressure Cooker XL will never leave you under pressure while cookingIf you think there is no way for you to whip up delicious, nutritious, and super flavorful meals with a single touch of a button, then you better think again because Power Pressure Cooker XL is about to become the definition of quick, effortless, and healthy cooking.

THE BENEFITS

So, why should you buy the Power Pressure Cooker XL? Besides the fact that the power pressure cooker XL has an incredible taste and flavor infusion technology that traps all the cooking flavors and keeps the intensity of the taste, here are some other benefits that will definitely convince you why setting some money aside for this dream-come-true appliance of every homemaker is the best home investment to make this very instant.

It Saves Energy

Since pressure cookers require less time to prepare food, they use less energy to create equally delicious meals. Say goodbye to wasting your energy with your pots, pans, and burners, because once you start cooking with the Power Pressure Cooker XL, you will drastically cut back on used energy. That will not only keep more money in your pocket each month, but it will also keep your stove clean at all times – since you will rarely use it.

It is Time Efficient

The Power Pressure Cooker XL traps the heated steam that occurs inside the pot during the process of cooking and creates a high-pressure environment that contributes to quick cooking. But besides the fact that the steam and pressure will cook your meals seventy percent faster than your stove, the efficiency of the Power Pressure Cooker XL is also in the preparation method. Because it requires no other pans, skillets, or woks and uses a single-pot cooking method, the Power Pressure Cooker XL requires no special preparations. It cooks without too much hassle and will help you serve delicious meals in a snap.

It is Economical

Not only will the Power Pressure Cooker XL save you time and money from energy, it will also allow you to cook inexpensive food to such a juicy and delightful perfection as if you used the most expensive cuts of meat and not those chops that were on sale.

It Preserves the Nutrients

Unlike the meals cooked with most of the traditional cookware, the Power Pressure Cooker XL leaves the nutrients intact. Due to the steam and pressure flow going on inside the Power Pressure Cooker XL during the cooking process, the food preserves its moisture and juiciness even after being cooked. The high-pressure environment locks in all the precious vitamins and nutrients, which means healthier and more nutritious meals for your dinner table.

It Does Not Expose You to Harmful Substances

It is not uncommon that most cooking methods do not only deprive the foods of their wholesomeness and destroys the vitamins, minerals and other nutrients during the process of cooking, but they also create certain harmful compounds such as elements that cause cancer or elevate the blood pressure. This is yet another reason why you should choose to cook your meals with the Power Pressure Cooker XL. Cooking under such pressure, the food is not only able to preserve its nutrients, but it is also not being exposed to harmful compounds.

It Has A Canning Option

Unlike the Instant Pot or other pressure cookers, this amazing, extra-large kitchen appliance comes with the option for canning and preserving food. If you love using those extra fruits and veggies for creating some yummy canned goods, then this is definitely the way to do it.

THE BUTTONS

If you are a proud owner of a new and shiny Power Pressure Cooker XL, you may be a little bit intimidated by the number of buttons found on the front of the cooker. Do not let its multi-functionality overwhelm you. The buttons aren't there to be overwhelming but to actually make the cooking experience a lot more convenient for you. Once you start cooking and really feel how every button works, I promise you, you won't even think about turning on your stove.

Here are the Power Pressure Cooker XL buttons and how to use them:

Delay Timer – This magical little option actually allows you to delay the cooking process. That means that you can set your pressure cooker later in the day. For instance, if you want to have a warm dinner waiting for you after you get home from work, all you have to do is simply whip up the meal, place it in the Power Pressure Cooker XL, and enter when you want it to start cooking. That way you can have a warm pot roast right after work without wasting 45 minutes to cook it. Amazing, right?

Canning/Preserving – If you love canned goods, you will absolutely love this option. Canning at 12 psi (the highest pressure allowed), you can not only preserve food, but you can also use it for cooking if your recipe requires a cooking time longer than 10 minutes.

Soup/Stew – This option for making soups and stews have a recommended setting for cooking time of ten minutes. That means if you press this button, it will pressure cook your food for ten minutes only. However, this button also allows you to use the cook time selector and adjust the cooking time anywhere from thirty to sixty minutes.

Slow Cook – Although this is a pressure cooker, the Power Pressure Cooker XL can also replace a slow cooker as well. If you want to slow cook a meal, all you have to do is choose the slow cook option. The manual setting here is two hours, but you can adjust it to six or twelve hours if you need to.

Rice/Risotto – The Power Pressure Cooker XL recommends that if you are cooking rice, you do it with this option. It has a manual setting for cooking for six minutes; however, you can adjust the cooking time anywhere from eighteen to twenty-five minutes. In fact, you will find that the manual recommends cooking white rice for six minutes, brown rice for eighteen minutes, and wild rice for twenty-five minutes.

Beans/Lentils – If you are making chili or cooking beans, lentils, or similar meals, you can easily do it with this option, since its manual setting is already adjusted for five minutes cook time. However, since you may need more time to cook your beans, depending on the type you are using, you can adjust the cooking time from fifteen to thirty minutes.

Fish/Vegetable/Steam – This button has the shortest manual setting for two minutes cook time. You can adjust it with the cook time selector from four to ten minutes.

Chicken/Meat – The manual setting is fifteen minutes cook time; however, you can easily adjust it to cook your meat to perfection. Since the Power Pressure Cooker XL does not have a manual button such as the Instant Pot, I find this one to be a pretty good manual replacement. With a great manual setting, this button will not only allow you to cook meat but any kind of food you want. As you will see later in the recipes, I use this button quite a lot.

Time Adjustment – If the manual setting of the buttons doesn't offer you the right cooking option for the meal you are preparing, you can adjust it with this button. Although there are many pre-adjusted options available to choose from, this button will allow you to manually choose the cooking pressure and time.

Keep Warm/Cancel – If you want to cancel a certain function or turn off the Power Pressure Cooker XL, you just need to press this button. After the cooking time ends, the Power Pressure Cooker XL will automatically switch to the Keep Warm option in order to keep your meals fresh and warm until ready to serve.

COOKING TIPS

The Power Pressure Cooker XL is not your regular kitchen appliance. It is in fact so versatile and multi-functional and is basically a combination of many other appliances:

- A pressure cooker
- A slow cooker
- A sautéing pan and stove top
- A rice cooker
- A steamer
- A warming pot

If you have all these appliances crowding your kitchen, replacing some of them with the Power Pressure Cooker XL is definitely the best choice.

However, it is its very versatility that intimidates people. If you are one of the many that simply cannot figure out how to get the most out of this device, then you might want to pay attention to these revolutionary tips:

- You can cook frozen food without defrosting. All you have to do is simply add a couple of minutes to your cooking time.
- Do not force open the lid. You must allow the pressure to be fully released before opening the lid. If the lid won't open, don't worry, it isn't stuck. That is just an indication that the Power Pressure Cooker XL is still pressurized and it isn't safe to open the lid. Allow a few more minutes and try again.
- The Power Pressure Cooker XL is extremely safe to use, but only if you use it right. The best way to ensure you will stay safe during releasing pressure and opening the lid is by ensuring that the venting knob is turned to the venting position and by tilting the lid away from you when opening.
- The Power Pressure Cooker XL does not have a sautéing or browning function. With this appliance you can easily sauté food by choosing any

of the given cooking options and cooking with the lid open. This makes the Power Pressure Cooker XL even more functional.

- Make sure not to overfill the Power Pressure Cooker XL. This will only increase the pressure and may even clog the valve. For best results, fill your Power Pressure Cooker XL until it is 2/3 full. However, if you are cooking food that may rise or expand during the cooking process, fill it only halfway.
- Do not use too much liquid. Always follow the recipes until you have gained some experience and can create delicious recipes on your own. If you add more liquid than necessary, this will not only give your meals that 'rinsed' taste and dilute the flavor, but it will also increase the time needed for the Power Pressure Cooker XL to go to pressure.

THE PRESSURE RELEASE

Luckily for every new user, the pressure valve of the Power Pressure Cooker XL has some pretty visible and easy-to-figure-out signs. If you line up the circle symbol, you will lock the pressure in, and if you choose to line up the symbol of the steam coming out, you are about to release the pressure.

Now, as to when you should use the quick and when the natural pressure release method, here is what you should know.

Quick – The quick pressure release method means allowing the steam to come out quickly. There really isn't a rule, and you can basically use this method anytime. However, you do have to keep in mind that if the Power Pressure Cooker XL is filled with liquid and you release the steam quickly, spillage will most likely occur.

This method is best to use after cooking meat, seafood, or veggies.

Natural – The natural pressure release method means just the opposite – allowing the steam to come out slowly. This method is best after cooking content that is starch-high, foamy food, or food with a large liquid volume.

COOKING TIMES

It would be remiss not to mention this, I know, but since there is detailed information about the cooking time found in your Power Pressure Cooker XL manual, I will briefly explain the basics.

Here is how long you should cook food in your Power Pressure Cooker XL:

Fresh Fish– ready after only two minutes of cooking

Vegetables – ready after only two minutes of cooking

Chili – usual cooking time is thirty minutes

Beef Roast – usual cooking time is thirty-five – forty minutes

Pork Roast – usual cooking time is forty – forty-five minutes

Whole Chicken – usual cooking time is twenty minutes

Juicy Ribs – usual cooking time is twenty minutes

Soup Recipes

Quick Beef Soup

Serves: 5

Prep + Cook time: 40 minutes

Ingredients:

2 lb. lean beef, chopped into bite-sized pieces

1 small onion, peeled and sliced

2 carrots, sliced

1 tsp of cayenne pepper

¼ tsp of black pepper, crushed

1 garlic clove, crushed

1 tbsp of butter

5 cups of water

Preparation:

Melt the butter on CHICKEN/MEAT settings with the lid open. Add onions and garlic. Stir-fry for 3 minutes, or until translucent. Add carrots and spices. Continue to cook for 2 more minutes.

Now, add the meat and pour in the water. Close the lid and set the timer to 35 minutes and cook on high pressure.

When done, press CANCEL button and release the steam naturally.

Nutrition information per serving:

Calories: 375, Protein: 55.5g, Carbs: 4.2g, Fats: 13.7g

Skim and Fast Miso and Tofu Soup

Serves: 4

Prep + Cook time: 12 minutes

Ingredients:

4 cups Water

½ cup Corn

2 tbsp Miso Paste

1 Onion, sliced

1 tsp Wakame Flakes

1 cup Silken Tofu, cubed

2 Celery Stalks, chopped

2 Carrots, chopped

Soy Sauce, to taste

Preparation:

Combine all the ingredients except the miso paste and soy sauce in your pressure cooker.

Close the lid and cook for 7 minutes on CHICKEN/MEAT. Release the pressure quickly.

Mix the miso paste with one cup of the broth and stir it into the soup. Add some soy sauce and stir.

Nutrition information per serving:

Calories 46, Carbohydrates 3.7 g, Fiber 1 g, Fat 1.7 g, Protein 3.8 g

Chicken Enchilada Soup

Serves: 4

Prep + Cook time: 15 minutes

Ingredients:

½ cup Salsa Verde

2 cups cooked and shredded Chicken

2 cups Chicken or Bone Broth

1 cup shredded Cheddar Cheese

4 ounces Cream Cheese

Preparation:

Combine the cream cheese, salsa, and broth in a food processor. Pulse until smooth. Transfer the mixture to a pressure cooker and heat on BEANS/LENTILS setting, lid off.

Cook until hot, but do not bring to a boil. Add the chicken and cook for about 4-5 minutes, or until it is heated through.

Serve immediately and enjoy!

Nutrition information per serving:

Calories 346, Net Carbs 3 g, Fat 23 g, Protein 25 g

Spring Spinach Soup

Serves: 5

Prep + Cook time: 45 minutes

Ingredients:

1 lb. lamb shoulder, cut into bite-sized pieces

11 oz. fresh spinach leaves, torn

3 eggs, beaten

4 cups of vegetable broth

2 tbsp of extra virgin olive oil

1 tsp of salt

Preparation:

Rinse the meat and pat dry with a paper towel. Cut into bite-sized pieces and set aside.

Rinse and drain each spinach leaf. Cut into bite-sized pieces. Place in your Power Pressure Cooker XL along with all other ingredients.

Set the steam release handle. Press SOUP button and cook for 30 minutes. Press CANCEL and release the steam handle. Turn off the cooker and set aside to chill for 10 minutes before serving.

Nutrition information per serving:

Calories: 325, Protein: 34.6g, Carbs: 3.4g, Fats: 19g

Chicken Soup

Serves: 4

Prep + Cook time: 35 minutes

Ingredients:

1 lb. organic chicken meat, dark and white pieces

1 tsp of salt

4 cups of chicken broth

½ cup of soup noodles

A handful of fresh parsley

¼ tsp of freshly ground black pepper

Preparation:

Using a sharp cutting knife, cut chicken into bite-sized pieces. Sprinkle with salt and place in the cooker. Pour in chicken broth and seal the lid. Set the steam release handle and press the SOUP button. Cook for 20 minutes and then press CANCEL. Release the pressure naturally and open the lid.

Now add soup noodles and close the lid again. Press the SOUP button and set the steam release handle. Cook for 5 more minutes.

Release the pressure naturally and open the lid. Sprinkle with some freshly ground black pepper and parsley.

Nutrition information per serving:

Calories: 282, Protein: 38.6g, Carbs: 6g, Fats: 10.2g

Poultry Recipes

Tender Chicken with Mushrooms

Serves: 3

Prep + Cook time: 25 minutes

Ingredients:

1 tbsp olive oil

1 lb. chicken breasts, skinless, boneless and cut into bite-sized pieces

1 garlic cloves, finely chopped

1 cup button mushrooms, chopped

2 cups chicken broth

1 tbsp all-purpose flour

1 tsp cayenne pepper, ground

¼ tsp black pepper, ground

Preparation:

Grease the cooker with some oil. Add garlic and meat, season with salt and stir-fry for 3 minutes. Add mushrooms and chicken broth. Seal the lid and adjust the steam release handle. Cook for 8 minutes on CHICKEN/MEAT setting.

When done, press CANCEL button and release the steam naturally.

Remove the lid and stir in flour, cayenne, and black pepper. Cook for 5 more minutes, with the cooker's lid off, on CHICKEN/MEAT, stirring constantly.

Nutrition information per serving:

Calories: 382, Protein: 48.4g, Carbs: 6.3g, Fats: 17g

Simple Dijon Chicken Thighs

Serves: 4

Prep + Cook time: 30 minutes

Ingredients:

½ cup Chicken Stock

1 tbsp. Olive Oil

½ cup chopped Onion

4 Chicken Thighs

¼ cup Heavy Cream

2 tbsp. Dijon Mustard

1 tsp Thyme

1 tsp Garlic Powder

Preparation:

Heat the olive oil on CHICKEN/MEAT mode. Brown the chicken for about 5-6 minutes per side. Set aside.

Sauté the onions inside the pressure cooker, add the stock, and simmer for 5 minutes.

Stir in mustard and cream, along with thyme and garlic powder. Pour the sauce over the chicken.

Nutrition information per serving:

Calories 528, Net Carbs 4 g, Fat 42 g, Protein 33 g

Mediterranean Chicken Breast

Serves: 2

Prep + Cook time: 15 minutes

Ingredients:

1 lb. Chicken Breast, sliced into half-inch thick filets

1 cup Olive Oil

½ cup freshly squeezed Lime juice

½ cup Parsley leaves, finely chopped

3 Garlic Cloves, crushed

1 tbsp Cayenne Pepper

1 tsp dried Oregano

1 tsp Sea Salt

Preparation:

In a medium-sized bowl, combine olive oil with lime juice, chopped parsley, crushed garlic, cayenne pepper, oregano, and salt.

Submerge the filets in this mixture and cover. Refrigerate for 30 minutes. Remove the meat from the refrigerator and transfer to the pressure cooker.

Close the lid. Press CHICKEN/MEAT button and set the timer to 7 minutes. When done, press CANCEL button and release the steam naturally.

Nutrition information per serving:

Calories: 325, Protein: 13.7g, Carbs: 5.3g, Fats: 29.2g

Creamy Turkey and Mushrooms

Serves: 4

Prep + Cook time: 40 minutes

Ingredients:

20 ounces Turkey Breasts, boneless and skinless

6 ounces White Button Mushrooms, sliced

3 tbsp chopped Shallots

½ tsp dried Thyme

½ cup dry White Wine

1 cup Chicken Stock

1 Garlic Clove, minced

2 tbsp Olive Oil

3 tbsp Heavy Cream

1 ½ tbsp Cornstarch

Salt and Pepper, to taste

Preparation:

Tie the turkey breast with a kitchen string horizontally, leaving approximately 2 inches apart. Season with salt and pepper.

Heat half of the olive oil in your Power Pressure Cooker XL. Add the turkey and cook for about 3 minutes on each side. Transfer to a plate.

Heat the remaining oil and cook shallots, thyme, garlic, and mushrooms until soft. Add white wine and scrape up the brown bits from the bottom.

When the alcohol evaporates, return the turkey to the pressure cooker. Close the lid and cook for 22 minutes on CHICKEN/MEAT.

Combine the heavy cream and cornstarch in a small bowl. Open the lid and stir in the mixture. Bring the sauce to a boil, then turn the cooker off.

Slice the turkey in half and serve topped with the creamy mushroom sauce.

Nutrition information per serving:

Calories 192, Carbohydrates 5 g, Fiber 1 g, Fat 12 g, Protein 15 g

Simple Pressure Cooked Whole Chicken

Serves: 4

Prep + Cook time: 40 minutes

Ingredients:

2-pound Whole Chicken

2 tbsp Olive Oil

1 ½ cups Water

Salt and Pepper, to taste

Preparation:

Rinse the chicken and pat dry. Season with salt and pepper.

Heat the oil in your Power Pressure Cooker XL and cook the chicken until browned on all sides.

Add a rack inside your pressure cooker and pour the water inside.

Place the chicken on the rack. Close the lid and cook for 25 minutes on CHICKEN/MEAT.

Nutrition information per serving:

Calories 376, Carbohydrates 1 g, Fiber 0 g, Fat 30 g, Protein 25.1 g

Fall-Off-Bone Drumsticks

Serves: 3

Prep + Cook time: 45 minutes

Ingredients:

1 tbsp Olive Oil

6 Skinless Chicken Drumsticks

4 Garlic Cloves, smashed

½ Red Bell Pepper, diced

½ Onion, diced

2 tbsp Tomato Paste

2 cups Water

Preparation:

Heat the olive oil in Power Pressure Cooker. Add onion and bell pepper and cook for about 4 minutes.

Add garlic and cook until it becomes golden. Combine the tomato paste with water and pour it into the Power Pressure Cooker.

Arrange the drumstick inside. Close the lid and cook for about 15 minutes on CHICKEN/MEAT.

Release the pressure naturally.

Nutrition information per serving:

Calories 454, Carbohydrates 6.7 g, Fiber 1.4 g, Fat 27.2 g, Protein 43.2 g

Creamy and Garlicky Italian Spinach Chicken

Serves: 4

Prep + Cook time: 15 minutes

Ingredients:

1 cup chopped Spinach

2 pounds Chicken Breasts, boneless and skinless, cut in half

½ cup Chicken Broth

2 Garlic Cloves, minced

2 tbsp Olive Oil

¾ cup Heavy Cream

½ cup Sun-Dried Tomatoes

2 tsp Italian Seasoning

½ cup Parmesan Chicken

½ tsp Salt

Preparation:

Rub the meat with the oil, garlic, salt, and seasonings. Add the chicken in your Power Pressure Cooker XL and brown it on all sides on CHICKEN/MEAT setting.

Pour the broth in, close the lid, and cook for 4 minutes. Release the pressure quickly and add the cream. Simmer for 5 minutes with the lid off, then stir in the cheese.

Stir in tomatoes and spinach and cook until the spinach wilts.

Nutrition information per serving:

Calories 455, Carbohydrates 3 g, Fiber 2 g, Fat 26 g, Protein 57 g

Garlic Chicken Breast

Serves: 4

Prep + Cook time: 25 minutes

Ingredients:

1 tbsp Olive Oil

2 pounds Chicken Breast, boneless and skinless

4 cups Chicken Broth

2 Garlic Cloves, crushed

1 medium-sized Onion, peeled and finely chopped

½ tablespoon Garlic Powder

Salt to taste

Preparation::

With the cooker's lid off, press BEANS/LENTILS mode and heat 1 tablespoon of olive oil. Add the chopped onion and stir-fry for about 2 minutes.

Add crushed garlic and stir well again. Cook for 2 minutes.

Add other ingredients and sprinkle salt to taste. Securely lock the cooker's lid and set for 15 minutes on CHICKEN/MEAT mode.

Perform a quick release to release the cooker's pressure.

Nutrition information per serving:

Calories: 259, Protein: 43.8g, Carbs: 4.1g, Fats: 6g

Ginger Chicken

Serves: 4

Prep + Cook time: 35 minutes

Ingredients:

1 lb. Chicken Thighs, skin and bones should be left on

1 tablespoon Chili Powder

1 tsp fresh Basil

¼ tsp Black Pepper, freshly ground

2 cups Chicken Broth

1 tbsp Ginger, freshly grated

1 tbsp Coriander Seeds

4 Garlic Cloves, crushed

Preparation::

Place all ingredients in your Power Pressure Cooker XL and set the steam release handle. Press CHICKEN/MEAT button and adjust the time to 25 minutes.

When you hear the cooker's end signal, perform a natural release and open the lid. Serve immediately.

Nutrition information per serving:

Calories: 313, Protein: 45.8g, Carbs: 3g, Fats: 11.9g

Chicken Wings with Ginger

Serves: 4

Prep + Cook time: 12 minutes

Ingredients:

2 lb. Chicken Wings

¼ cup Extra Virgin Olive Oil

4 Garlic Cloves, crushed

1 tbsp Rosemary leaves

½ tsp White Pepper

½ tsp Cayenne Pepper

½ tbsp fresh Thyme, finely chopped

½ tbsp fresh Ginger, grated

¼ cup Lime juice

½ cup Apple Cider Vinegar

Preparation:

In a large bowl, combine olive oil with garlic, rosemary, white pepper, cayenne pepper, thyme, ginger, lime juice, and apple cider vinegar. Submerge wings into this mixture and cover. Refrigerate for 1 hour.

Remove the wings from the marinade and pat dry with a paper towel. Plug in your pressure cooker and place the chicken inside. Close the lid and adjust steam release handle. Set the timer to 8 minutes and cook on CHICKEN/MEAT mode. When done, press CANCEL button and release the steam naturally.

Nutrition information per serving:

Calories: 482, Protein: 66.1g, Carbs: 3.5g, Fats: 20.6g

Meat Recipes

Butter Veal Chops

Serves: 4

Prep + Cook time: 55 minutes

Ingredients:

2 tbsp of Butter

1.5 lb. boneless Veal Shoulder, cut into bite-sized pieces

2 Tomatoes, roughly chopped

1 tbsp of All-purpose Flour

1/2 tbsp of Cayenne Pepper

1 tbsp of Parsley, finely chopped

Preparation:

Grease the pressure cooker with 1 tbsp of butter. Make a layer with veal chops and pour enough water to cover. Season with salt and close the lid. Set the steam release handle and press CHICKEN/MEAT button. Set the timer for 45 minutes. When done, perform a quick release and let it stand covered for a while.

Meanwhile, melt the remaining butter in a small skillet. Add 1 tablespoon of cayenne pepper, one tablespoon of all-purpose flour, and stir-fry for about 2 minutes. Remove from the heat.

Place the meat and tomatoes on a serving plate. Drizzle with browned cayenne pepper and sprinkle with chopped parsley. Serve immediately.

Nutrition information per serving:

Calories: 437, Protein: 49.7g, Carbs: 2.3g, Fats: 21.8g

Shredded Beef the Caribbean Way

Serves: 4

Prep + Cook time: 1 hour

Ingredients:

2 pounds Beef Roast

½ tsp Turmeric

1 tsp grated Ginger

¼ cup Water

4 whole Garlic Cloves

1 tsp dried Thyme

1 tsp Garlic Powder

Preparation:

Combine the turmeric, garlic, thyme, and ginger in a small bowl. Rub the mixture into the beef.

Stick the cloves into the beef roast. Place the beer inside your Power Pressure Cooker and pour the water around it.

Cook for about 50 minutes on CHICKEN/MEAT mode. Shred the meat.

Nutrition information per serving:

Calories 739.2, Carbohydrates 1.3 g, Fiber 0.2 g, Fat 56.7 g, Protein 56.9 g

Port Wine Garlicky Lamb

Serves: 4

Prep + Cook time: 30 minutes

Ingredients:

2 pounds Lamb Shanks

1 tbsp Olive Oil

½ cup Port Wine

1 tbsp Tomato Paste

10 Garlic Cloves, peeled

½ cup Chicken Broth

1 tsp Balsamic Vinegar

½ tsp dried Rosemary

1 tbsp Butter

Preparation:

Heat the oil in your Power Pressure Cooker and brown the lamb shanks on all sides. Add the garlic and cook them until lightly browned. Stir in the rest of the ingredients, except the butter and vinegar.

Close the lid and cook for 20 – 25 minutes (depending on the preferred density) on CHICKEN/MEAT mode. Release the pressure naturally.

Remove the lamb shanks and let the sauce boil for 5 minutes with the lid off. Stir in the vinegar and butter. Serve the gravy poured over the shanks.

Nutrition information per serving:

Calories 620, Carbohydrates 8.7 g, Fiber 0.5 g, Fat 34.9 g, Protein 60 g

Smokey Pork Roast

Serves: 4

Prep + Cook time: 1 hour and 15 minutes

Ingredients:

2 pounds Pork Meat by choice

1 tsp Oregano

1 tsp Cumin

1 tsp Liquid Smoke

1 tsp Coconut Sugar

1 tbsp Coconut Oil

1 tsp ground Ginger

½ cup Beef Broth

1 tsp Paprika

½ tsp Pepper

Preparation:

Place all the spices in a small bowl and stir to combine. Rub the meat with the spice mixture. Melt the coconut oil in your Power Pressure Cooker XL.

Add the pork and cook until browned on all sides. Combine the liquid smoke and broth and pour over the pork.

Close the lid and cook for about 45 minutes on CHICKEN/MEAT mode. Let the pressure release naturally.

Nutrition information per serving:

Calories 767, Carbohydrates 2.2 g, Fiber 0.5 g, Fat 41.9 g, Protein 89 g

Herbed Lamb Roast with Potatoes

Serves: 4

Prep + Cook time: 30 minutes

Ingredients:

6 pounds Leg of Lamb

1 tsp dried Sage

1 tsp dried Marjoram

1 Bay Leaf, crushed

1 tsp dried Thyme

3 Garlic Cloves, minced

3 pounds Potatoes, cut into pieces

2 tbsp Olive Oil

3 tbsp Arrowroot Powder

1/3 cup Water

2 cups Chicken Broth

Preparation:

Heat the oil in your Power Pressure Cooker. Combine the herbs with some salt and pepper and rub the mixture into the meat. Brown the lamb on all sides.

Pour the broth around the meat, close the lid, and cook for 60 minutes on CHICKEN/MEAT. Release the pressure quickly and add the potatoes.

Close the lid and cook for 12 more minutes. Transfer the meat and potatoes to a plate. Combine the water and arrowroot and stir the mixture into the pot sauce. Pour the gravy over the meat and potatoes and enjoy.

Nutrition information per serving:

Calories 739.2, Carbohydrates 1.3 g, Fiber 0.2 g, Fat 56.7 g, Protein 56.9 g

Black Pepper Beef

Serves: 6

Prep + Cook time: 45 minutes

Ingredients:

2 tbsp Vegetable Oil

4 medium-sized Onions, peeled and finely chopped

4 Garlic Cloves, peeled and finely crushed

2 lb. lean Beef, chopped into bite-sized pieces

1 tsp Salt

1 tsp freshly ground Black Pepper, to taste

1 tsp Cayenne Pepper

1 tbsp Tomato Sauce

Preparation:

Heat the oil on BEANS/LENTILS mode. Add chopped onions, garlic, and stir-fry for 2-3 minutes.

Now add the meat, salt, pepper, cayenne pepper, and tomato sauce. Mix well and pour enough water to cover the ingredients. Securely lock the cooker's lid and set for 20 minutes on the CHICKEN/MEAT mode.

Nutrition information per serving:

Calories: 384, Protein: 47.2g, Carbs: 3g, Fats: 16.4g

Jerk Pork Pot Roast

Serves: 12

Prep + Cook time: 4 hours and 20 minutes

Ingredients:

4-pound Pork Roast

1 tbsp. Olive Oil

¼ cup Jerk Spice Blend

½ cup Beef Stock

Preparation:

Rub the pork with olive oil and the spice blend.

Sear the meat well on all sides on CHICKEN/MEAT mode. Add the beef broth.

Cover the cooker, reduce the heat, and let cook for 4 hours on SLOW COOK mode.

Nutrition information per serving:

Calories 282, Net Carbs 0 g, Fat 24 g, Protein 23 g

Salisbury Steak

Serves: 6

Prep + Cook time: 25 minutes

Ingredients:

2 pounds Ground Chuck

1 tbsp. Onion Flakes

1 ½ tsp Salt

1 tsp Pepper

¾ Almond Flour

¼ cup Beef Broth

1 tbsp. chopped Parsley

1 tbsp. Worcestershire Sauce

Preparation:

Combine all the ingredients in a bowl. Mix well with your hands and make 6 patties out of the mixture.

Arrange on a lined baking sheet. Cook on CHICKEN/MEAT for about 20 minutes.

Nutrition information per serving:

Calories 354, Net Carbs 2.5 g, Fat 28 g, Protein 27 g

Red Pepper Beef Steak

Serves: 3

Prep + Cook time: 55 minutes

Ingredients:

3 1½-inch thick Rib-eye Steak, boneless

2 tbsp freshly squeezed Lemon juice

3 tbsp Canola Oil

3 tbsp Dijon Mustard

½ tsp freshly ground Black Pepper

3 cups Beef Broth

Preparation:

Remove the steaks from the refrigerator 20 minutes before cooking. Cover and let them sit at room temperature.

In a small bowl, combine lemon juice, oil, mustard, salt, and pepper. Brush the steaks with this mixture and set aside.

Pour the beef broth in the pressure cooker. Place the steamer insert and arrange the steaks. Seal the lid and press the STEAM. Cook for 35 minutes. Perform a quick release and open the lid.

Remove the broth and press the CHICKEN/MEAT button. Brown steaks on both sides for 3-4 minutes.

Nutrition information per serving:

Calories: 568, Protein: 30.6g, Carbs: 1g, Fats: 48.5g

Fish and Seafood Recipes

Trout Filet

Serves: 6

Prep + Cook time: 75 minutes

Ingredients:

2 lb. Trout Filets, skin on

½ cup Olive Oil

¼ cup Apple Cider Vinegar

1 red Onion, sliced

1 Lemon, sliced

2 Garlic Cloves, crushed

1 tbsp fresh Rosemary, chopped

1 tbsp Dill Sprigs, chopped

½ Sea Salt

¼ tsp freshly ground Black Pepper

3 cups Fish Stock

Preparation:

In a medium-sized bowl, combine olive oil with apple cider, sliced onions, crushed garlic, rosemary, dill, sea salt, and pepper. Submerge the filets into this mixture and refrigerate for 1 hour.

Remove the fish from the refrigerator. Grease the bottom of the cooker with some of the marinade, 3-4 tablespoons, and pour in fish stock.

Add the fish and seal the lid. Set the steam release handle and press the FISH/ STEAM button. Cook for 5 minutes.

When you hear the cooker's end signal, perform a quick release and open the lid.

Grease a large, non-stick skillet with the remaining marinade and heat over medium-high heat. Briefly brown the filets on both sides, 2-3 minutes is enough.

Nutrition information per serving:

Calories: 373, Protein: 32.6g, Carbs: 3.9g Fats: 25g

Crab Cakes

Serves: 6

Prep + Cook time: 15 minutes

Ingredients:

2 tbsp. Coconut Oil

1 tbsp. Lemon Juice

1 cup Lump Crab Meat

2 tbsp. Parsley

2 tsp Dijon Mustard

1 Egg, beaten

1 ½ tbsp. Coconut Flour

Preparation:

Check to make sure there are no shells left in the crab meat and place it in a bowl. Add the remaining ingredients, except coconut oil.

Mix well to combine. Make 6 crab cakes out of the mixture.

Melt the coconut oil in the power pressure cooker xl. Add the crab cakes and cook for about 2-3 minutes per side on BEANS/LENTILS.

Nutrition information per serving:

Calories 65, Net Carbs 3.6 g, Fat 5 g, Protein 5.3 g

Nutty Seabass

Serves: 2

Prep + Cook time: 30 minutes

Ingredients:

2 Sea Bass Filets

2 tbsp. Butter

½ tsp Salt, Pepper

1/3 cup roasted Hazelnuts

Pinch of Cayenne Pepper

Preparation:

Line a baking paper or on the rack with waxed paper.

Melt the butter and brush it over the fish. In a food processor, combine the rest of the ingredients.

Coat the sea bass with the hazelnut mixture. Place it on the paper and cook for about 15 minutes on STEAM/FISH mode.

Nutrition information per serving:

Calories 467, Net Carbs 2.8 g, Fat 31 g, Protein 40 g

Clams in White Wine

Serves: 4

Prep + Cook time: 17 minutes

Ingredients:

¼ cup White Wine

2 cups Veggie Broth

¼ cup chopped Basil

¼ cup Olive Oil

2 ½ pounds Clams

2 tbsp Lemon Juice

2 Garlic Cloves, minced

Preparation:

Heat the olive oil in your Power Pressure Cooker. Add garlic and cook for one minute.

Add wine, basil, lemon juice, and veggie broth. Bring the mixture to a boil and boil for one minute.

Add your steaming basket and place the clams inside. Close the lid and cook for 4 minutes on STEAM/FISH mode.

Place the clams on a plate and drizzle with the cooking liquid.

Nutrition information per serving:

Calories 224.4, Carbohydrates 5.8 g, Fiber 0.1 g, Fat 14.6 g, Protein 15.6 g

Almond-Crusted Tilapia

Serves: 4

Prep + Cook time: 10 minutes

Ingredients:

4 Tilapia Filets

2/3 cup sliced Almonds

1 cup Water

2 tbsp Dijon Mustard

1 tsp Olive Oil

¼ tsp Black Pepper

Preparation:

Pour the water in your Power Pressure Cooker. Mix the olive oil, pepper, and mustard in a small bowl.

Brush the fish filets with the mustard mixture on all sides. Coat the fish in almonds slices.

Place the rack in your Power Pressure Cooker and arrange the fish filets on it. Close the lid and cook for 5 minutes on STEAM/FISH.

Do a quick pressure release.

Nutrition information per serving:

Calories 326.8, Carbohydrates 4.1 g, Fiber 2.8 g, Fat 14.9 g, Protein 46.1 g

Mediterranean Salmon

Serves: 4

Prep + Cook time: 15 minutes

Ingredients:

4 frozen Salmon Filets

2 tbsp Olive Oil

1 Rosemary Sprig

1 cup Cherry Tomatoes

15 ounces Asparagus

1 cup Water

Preparation:

Pour the water in your Power Pressure Cooker and insert the rack.

Place the salmon on the rack, top with rosemary, and arrange the asparagus on top. Close the lid and cook on STEAM/FISH for 2 minutes.

Add the cherry tomatoes on top and cook for 2 more minutes. Serve drizzled with olive oil.

Nutrition information per serving

Calories 475.6 Carbohydrates 6.3 g, Fiber 2.7 g, Fat 31.5 g, Protein 42.9 g

Wrapped Fish and Potatoes

Serves: 4

Prep + Cook time: 15 minutes

Ingredients:

4 Fish Filets

4 Thyme Sprigs

2 Potatoes, sliced

1 Lemon, sliced thinly

1 Onion, sliced

A Handful of Fresh Parsley

2 cups of Water

2 tbsp Olive Oil

Preparation:

Place each fish filet on parchment paper, separately. Divide the potatoes, thyme, parsley, onion, and lemon between the 4 parchment papers.

Drizzle each of them with ½ tbsp of olive oil and mix with your hands to coat everything.

Wrap the fish with the parchment paper. Wrap each of the 'packets' in aluminum foil. Pour the water in your Power Pressure Cooker.

Place the packets inside. If you are using a 6-quart Power Pressure Cooker you may need to cook 2 packets at a time. Close the lid and cook for about 5 minutes on BEANS/LENTILS mode.

Nutrition information per serving:

Calories 310, Carbohydrates 9 g, Fiber 3 g, Fat 14 g, Protein 30 g

Lemon Sauce Salmon

Serves: 4

Prep + Cook time: 10 minutes

Ingredients:

4 Salmon Filets

1 tbsp Honey

½ tsp Cumin

1 tbsp Hot Water

1 tbsp Olive Oil

1 tsp Smoked Paprika

1 tbsp chopped Fresh Parsley

¼ cup Lemon Juice

1 cup of Water

Preparation:

Pour the water inside your Power Pressure Cooker. Place the salmon filets on the rack.

Close the lid and cook for about 3 minutes on STEAM/FISH mode. Whisk together the remaining ingredients.

Release the pressure quickly, drizzle the sauce over the salmon. Close the lid and cook for 2 more minutes.

Nutrition information per serving:

Calories 493, Carbohydrates 6.3 g, Fiber 0.3 g, Fat 31.5 g, Protein 41.2 g

Cod in a Tomato Sauce

Serves: 4

Prep + Cook time: 15 minutes

Ingredients:

4 Cod Filets (7-oz. each)

2 cups chopped Tomatoes

1 cup of Water

1 tbsp Olive Oil

Salt and Pepper, to taste

¼ tsp Garlic Powder

Preparation:

Place the tomatoes in a baking dish and crush them with a fork. Season with some salt, pepper, and garlic powder.

Season the cod with salt and pepper and place it over the tomatoes. Drizzle the olive oil over the fish and tomatoes.

Place the dish in your Power Pressure Cooker. Close the lid and cook on STEAM/FISH for 5 minutes. Release the pressure naturally.

Nutrition information per serving:

Calories 251, Carbohydrates 3 g, Fiber 1 g, Fat 5.2 g, Protein 44.8 g

Garlic Salmon Steak

Serves: 3

Prep + Cook time: 60 minutes

Ingredients:

1 lb. wild Salmon Steaks

1 tsp Garlic Powder

½ tsp Rosemary Powder

1 cup Extra Virgin Olive Oil

½ cup Apple Cider Vinegar

¼ cup Lemon juice

½ tsp White Pepper

Preparation:

In a large bowl, combine garlic powder, rosemary powder, olive oil, apple cider vinegar, salt, lemon juice, and pepper. Pour the mixture into a Ziploc bag along with the salmon. Seal the bag and shake once or twice to coat the steaks with the marinade. Refrigerate for 30 minutes.

Pour in 3 cups of water in the pressure cooker and set the steamer insert. Remove the fish from the Ziploc bag and place on the steamer basket. Reserve the marinade.

Close the cooker's lid and set the steam release handle. Press FISH/STEAM button and cook for 15 minutes.

When you hear the cooker's end signal, perform a quick release and open the lid. Remove the steaks along with the steamer insert and liquid.

Rinse the stainless-steel insert and pat dry with a paper towel. Grease with some of the marinade and press the BEANS/LENTILS button.

Add salmon steaks and brown them on both sides, for 3-4 minutes.

Nutrition information per serving:

Calories: 304, Protein: 32g, Carbs: 2g, Fats: 18g

Basil and Rosemary Shrimp

Serves: 4

Prep + Cook time: 10 minutes

Ingredients:

1 lb. Shrimp, whole

½ cup Extra Virgin Olive Oil

1 tsp Garlic Powder

1 tsp dried Rosemary, crushed

1 tsp dried Thyme

½ tsp dried Basil

½ tsp dried Sage

½ tsp Cayenne Pepper

Preparation:

In a bowl, combine olive oil with garlic powder, rosemary, thyme, basil, sage, salt, and cayenne pepper.

Using a kitchen brush, spread the marinade over each shrimp. Transfer the shrimp into the pressure cooker. Close the lid and press FISH/STEAM button.

Adjust the steam release and cook for 3 minutes.

When done, press the CANCEL button and release the steam naturally. Press BEANS/LENTILS button and stir-fry for 2 more minutes, or until golden brown.

Nutrition information per serving:

Calories: 356, Protein: 26g, Carbs: 2.9g, Fats: 27.3g

Vegetarian Recipes

Crispy Leeks with Garlic

Serves: 3

Prep + Cook time: 15 minutes

Ingredients:

4 Leeks, cut into 2-inches long pieces

4 Garlic Cloves, crushed

1 tsp Sea Salt

¼ cup Extra Virgin Olive Oil

3 tbsp freshly squeezed Lemon juice

Preparation:

In a small bowl, combine olive oil with sea salt and garlic. Stir well and set aside.

Place the leeks in the pressure cooker. Drizzle oil mixture over the leeks and close the lid. Press FISH/STEAM button and cook for 3 minutes.

When done, press CANCEL button and turn off the cooker. Release the steam naturally. Transfer to a serving plate and sprinkle with freshly squeezed lemon juice.

Nutrition information per serving:

Calories: 246, Protein: 2.6g, Carbs: 5.3g, Fats: 17.4g

Fried Fake Mac and Cheese

Serves: 7

Prep + Cook time: 45 minutes

Ingredients:

1 Cauliflower Head, riced in a food processor

1 ½ cups shredded Cheese

2 tsp Paprika

¾ tsp Rosemary

2 tsp Turmeric

3 Eggs

Oil, for frying

Preparation:

Microwave the cauliflower for 5 minutes. Place it in cheesecloth and squeeze the extra juices out.

Place the cauliflower in a bowl. Stir in the rest of the ingredients.

Heat the oil on BEANS/LENTILS and add the 'mac and cheese' and fry until golden and crispy. Drain on paper towels before serving.

Nutrition information per serving:

Calories 160, Net Carbs 2 g, Fat 12 g, Protein 8.6 g

Fake Mushroom Risotto

Serves: 4

Prep + Cook time: 15 minutes

Ingredients:

2 Shallots, diced

3 tbsp. Olive Oil

¼ cup Veggie Broth

1/3 cup Parmesan Cheese

4 tbsp. Butter

3 tbsp. chopped Chives

2 pounds Mushrooms, sliced

4 ½ cups riced Cauliflower

Preparation:

Heat 2 tbsp. in the power pressure cooker XL on BEANS/LENTILS mode.

Add the mushrooms and cook for about 3 minutes. Remove from cooker and set aside. Heat the remaining oil and cook the shallots for 2 minutes.

Stir in the cauliflower and broth and cook until the liquid is absorbed. Stir in the rest of the ingredients and cook for another 2-3 minutes. Serve immediately.

Nutrition information per serving:

Calories 264, Net Carbs 6.4 g, Fat 18 g, Protein 11 g

Vegan Olive and Avocado Zoodles

Serves: 4

Prep + Cook time: 15 minutes

Ingredients:

4 Zucchini, julienned or spiralized (zoodles)

½ cup Paleo Pesto

2 Avocados, sliced

1 cup Kalamata Olives, chopped

¼ cup chopped Basil

2 tbsp. Olive Oil

¼ tsp Salt

¼ cup chopped Sun-dried Tomatoes

Preparation:

Heat half of the olive oil in the pressure cooker on BEANS/LENTILS mode. Add zoodles and cook for 4 minutes. Transfer to a plate.

Stir in olive oil, pesto, basil, salt, tomatoes, and olives. Top with avocado slices and serve.

Nutrition information per serving:

Calories 449, Net Carbs 8.4 g, Fat 42 g, Protein 6.3 g

Meatless Shepherd's Pie

Serves: 4

Prep + Cook time: 17 minutes

Ingredients:

½ cup diced Celery

1 cup diced Onion

2 cups steamed and mashed Cauliflower

1 tbsp Olive Oil

½ cup diced Turnip

1 ¾ cup Veggie Broth

1 cup diced Tomatoes

1 cup grated Potatoes

½ cup diced Carrot

Preparation:

Heat the olive oil in your Power Pressure Cooker. Add onions, carrots, and celery and cook for 3 minutes.

Stir in turnips, potatoes, and veggie broth. Close the lid and cook for 10 minutes BEANS/LENTILS setting. Stir in tomatoes.

Transfer the mixture to 4 ramekins. Top each ramekin with ½ cup of mashed cauliflower. Pour ½ cup of water inside the Power Pressure Cooker and place the trivet. Close the lid and cook for 5 minutes BEANS/LENTILS.

Nutrition information per serving:

Calories 224.4, Carbohydrates 5.8 g, Fiber 0.1 g, Fat 14.6 g, Protein 15.6 g

Eggs

Scrambled Eggs with Ground Beef

Serves: 3

Prep + Cook time: 20 minutes

Ingredients:

8 oz lean Ground Beef

1 Onion, finely chopped

3 Eggs

¼ cup Skim Milk

¼ cup fresh Goat's Cheese

¼ tsp Garlic Powder

¼ tsp Rosemary Powder

1 tbsp Tomato Paste

2 tbsp Olive Oil

Preparation:

Grease the pressure cooker with olive oil. Press BEANS/LENTILS button and add the onion. Stir-fry until translucent. Now, add beef and tomato paste. Continue to cook for 5 more minutes, stirring occasionally.

Meanwhile, whisk together eggs, milk, goat's cheese, rosemary powder, garlic powder, and salt. Pour the mixture into the pressure cooker and stir slowly with a wooden spatula. Cook until slightly underdone, around 10 minutes.

Nutrition information per serving:

Calories: 302, Protein: 27.5g, Carbs: 6.1g, Fats: 18.6g

Spinach Omelet

Serves: 2

Prep + Cook time: 20 minutes

Ingredients:

2 tbsp Olive Oil

1 cup Spinach, chopped

1 cup Swiss Chard, chopped

3 Eggs

1 tsp Garlic Powder

½ tsp Sea Salt

¼ tsp Red Pepper Flakes

Preparation:

Grease the pressure cooker's bottom with 2 tablespoons of olive oil. Press BEANS/LENTILS button and add greens. Stir-fry for 5 minutes. Remove from the cooker and set aside.

Whisk together eggs, garlic powder, salt, and red pepper flakes. Pour the mixture into the stainless-steel insert. Spread the eggs evenly with a wooden spatula and cook for about 2-3 minutes.

Using a spatula, ease around the edges and slide to a serving plate. Add greens and fold it over in half.

Nutrition information per serving:

Calories: 227, Protein: 9.3g, Carbs: 2.9g, Total Fats: 20.7g

Baked Avocado with Eggs

Serves: 2

Prep + Cook time: 30 minutes

Ingredients:

1 Avocado, sliced in half

2 Eggs, whole

3 tbsp Butter, melted

1 tsp dried Oregano

½ tsp Pink Himalayan Salt

Preparation:

Slice the avocado in half and brush with butter. Place in the steamer insert and gently crack the eggs. Season with salt and oregano. Add about 1 cup of water to the stainless-steel insert of your power pressure cooker xl.

Press STEAM button and cook for 20 minutes.

When done, press CANCEL button and turn off the cooker. Quickly open the lid. Carefully transfer the avocado to the serving plate.

Nutrition information per serving:

Calories: 423, Protein: 7.7g, Total Carb: 3.5g, Net Carbs: 2.4g Fats: 41.3g

Boiled Eggs with Spinach and Peanuts

Serves: 4

Prep + Cook time: 25 minutes

Ingredients:

3 cups of Water

1 lb Spinach, chopped

2 tbsp Olive Oil

1 tbsp Butter

4 Eggs

1 tbsp Mustard Seeds

1 tbsp Peanuts

½ tsp Chili Flakes

Preparation:

Pour 3 cups of water in the stainless-steel insert of the Power Pressure Cooker XL. Add eggs and close the lid. Adjust the steam release handle and press RICE/RISOTTO button. Cook for 5 minutes.

When done, press CANCEL button and perform a quick release. Open the lid and transfer the eggs into ice cold water.

Clean and pat dry the insert with paper towels and return it to the cooker. Grease with olive oil and press BEANS/LENTILS button. Add spinach and cook for 2-3 minutes, stirring occasionally.

Now, stir in 1 tablespoon of butter and season with salt and chili flakes. Mix well and cook for 1 more minute. Turn off the cooker and sprinkle with nuts.

Gently peel and slice each egg in half, lengthwise.

Nutrition information per serving:

Calories: 245, Protein: 10.5g, Total Carb: 6.6g, Net Carbs 3.1: Fats: 21.4g

Poached Eggs with Mushrooms

Serves: 1

Prep + Cook time: 25 minutes

Ingredients:

3 oz Button Mushrooms, sliced in half lengthwise

2 oz fresh Arugula

1 Egg

2 tbsp Olive Oil

Preparation:

Run the mushrooms under cold water. Pat dry with some paper towels, making sure to wipe away any extra debris. Using a sharp paring knife, slice each mushroom in half lengthwise, but keep the stems on. Set aside.

Plug in your pressure cooker and add butter to the stainless-steel insert. Press BEANS/LENTILS button and melt it.

Add mushrooms and cook for 4-5 minutes, or until the liquid evaporates. Now, add arugula and give it a good stir. Cook for 1 minute.

Finally, crack the egg and cook until set, for 2 minutes. Turn off the cooker and carefully transfer the omelet to a serving plate using a large spatula.

Nutrition information per serving:

Calories: 338, Protein: 10.1g, Carbs: 5.7g, Fats: 33g

Poached Eggs with Leeks

Serves: 3

Prep + Cook time: 15 minutes

Ingredients:

1 cup leeks, chopped into one-inch pieces

3 eggs

2 tbsp oil

1 tbsp butter

1 tsp Mustard Seeds

1 tbsp dried Rosemary

¼ tsp Chili Flakes

¼ tsp Salt

Preparation:

Rinse the leeks under cold running water. Drain in a large colander and place on a clean work surface. Using a sharp knife, cut into 1-inch long pieces. Set aside.

Plug in your power pressure cooker xl and grease the stainless-steel insert with olive oil. Press BEANS/LENTILS button and add mustard seeds. Stir-fry for 2-3 minutes.

Now, add leeks and butter. Cook for 5 minutes, stirring occasionally. Crack 3 eggs and season with dried rosemary, chili flakes, and salt.

Cook until set, for 4 minutes.

Nutrition information per serving:

Calories: 204, Protein: 6.4g, Total Carb: 5.6g, Net Carbs: 4.4g Fats: 17.9g

Poached Egg Vegetable Frittata

Serves: 5

Prep + Cook time: 30 minutes

Ingredients:

3 tbsp Oil

10 oz. Spinach, finely chopped

2 Cherry Tomatoes, halved

¼ cup Red Bell Pepper, chopped

1 cup chopped Broccoli, pre-cooked

5 Eggs

½ cup Cheddar Cheese

½ cup fresh Ricotta Cheese

½ cup fresh Celery leaves, finely chopped

Preparation:

Grease the pressure cooker with oil. Press BEANS/LENTILS button. Add spinach and give it a good stir. Cook for 5 minutes, stirring occasionally. Now add tomatoes, bell peppers, and broccoli. Continue to cook for 3-4 minutes.

In a small bowl, whisk together 2 eggs, cheddar, and ricotta. Add it to the cooker and cook for 2 more minutes. Finally, crack the remaining three eggs. Cook for another 5 minutes.

When done, turn off the cooker. Transfer to a serving plate and sprinkle with chopped celery leaves and salt.

Nutrition information per serving:

Calories: 240, Protein: 11.3g, Carbs: 5.3g, Fats: 20g

Scrambled Eggs with Cranberries

Serves: 2

Prep + Cook time: 7 minutes

Ingredients:

4 large Eggs, beaten

¼ tsp Powdered Stevia

¼ tsp Cranberry Extract, sugar-free

2 tbsp Butter

¼ tsp Salt

1 tbsp Skim Milk

4 Cranberries

Preparation:

In a large bowl, whisk together eggs, stevia, cranberry extract, salt, and milk.

Add butter to the pressure cooker. Press BEANS/LENTILS button and melt it. Pour the egg mixture and gently pull the eggs across the pot with a wooden spatula. Do not stir constantly. Cook for about 2 minutes, or until thickened and no visible liquid egg remains.

When done, turn off the cooker and transfer to a serving plate. Top with cranberries and garnish with some fresh mint.

Nutrition information per serving:

Calories: 248, Protein: 13g, Carbs: 1.2g, Fats: 21.5g

Poached Eggs with Spinach and Keto Pancakes

Serves: 2

Prep + Cook time: 20 minutes

Ingredients:

3 tbsp Oil

7 oz Spinach, chopped

½ tsp Sea Salt, divided

½ tsp Garlic Powder

2 Eggs

¼ tsp dried Oregano

¼ tsp dried Rosemary

Preparation:

Grease the stainless-steel insert with oil. Press BEANS/LENTILS button and add the chopped spinach. Season with salt and garlic powder. Give it a good stir and cook for 5 minutes.

Crack eggs and season with dried oregano, dried rosemary, and the remaining salt. Cook until completely set, for 5 more minutes.

Nutrition information per serving:

Calories: 269, Protein: 8.5g, Carbs: 4.7g, Fats: 25.2g

Kale Cheddar Cheese Omelet

Serves: 2

Prep + Cook time: 10 minutes

Ingredients:

4 Eggs

½ cup Cheddar Cheese, crumbled

1 small Onion, finely chopped

½ tsp Italian Seasoning mix

2 tsp Cooking Spray

1 tsp Salt

½ tsp Black Pepper, ground

2 tbsp Heavy Cream

Preparation:

In a large mixing bowl, combine eggs, salt, pepper, and heavy cream. Whisk until well combined and then add all the remaining ingredients. Whisk again and set aside.

Grease the stainless-steel insert of the pressure cooker xl with cooking spray. Pour in the egg mixture and press BEANS/LENTILS button. Adjust the steam release handle and set the timer to 5 minutes.

When done, press CANCEL button and release the pressure naturally.

Nutrition information per serving:

Calories: 370, Protein: 24.4g, Carbs: 5.4g, Fats: 25.2g

Steamed Eggs with Scallions

Serves: 1

Prep + Cook time: 10 minutes

Ingredients:

2 Eggs

1 tbsp Spring Onions, chopped

1 cup Water

¼ tsp Garlic Powder

½ tsp Salt

¼ tsp Black Pepper

Preparation:

In a medium bowl, combine eggs and water. Whisk well until combined. Using a small strainer, strain into heat proof bowl. Add the remaining ingredients and stir all well. Set aside.

Plug in your power pressure cooker xl and add 1 cup of water into the stainless-steel insert. Set the steamer insert and place the bowl onto the steamer. Close the lid and adjust the steam release handle. Press BEANS/LENTILS button and set the timer to 5 minutes.

When done, press CANCEL button and perform a quick release to release the pressure.

Nutrition information per serving:

Calories: 131, Protein: 11.4g, Carbs: 2g, Fats: 8.8g

Dessert Recipes

Crème Caramel Flan

Serves: 4

Prep + Cook time: 30 minutes

Ingredients:

2 Eggs

7 ounces Condensed Coconut Milk

½ cups Coconut Milk

1 ½ cups Water

½ tsp Vanilla

Preparation:

Place a pan with a heavy bottom in your Power Pressure Cooker. Place the sugar in the pan.

Cook until a caramel is formed. Divide the caramel between 4 small ramekins.

Pour the water in the pressure cooker and lower the trivet.

Beat the rest of the ingredients together and divide them between the ramekins. Cover them with aluminum foil and place in the Power Pressure Cooker.

Close the lid and cook for 5 minutes on CHICKEN/MEAT. Release the pressure naturally.

Nutrition information per serving:

Calories 107.8, Carbohydrates 16.5 g, Fiber 0 g, Fat 3.3 g, Protein 3.3 g

Simple Keto Sherbet

Serves: 1

Prep + Cook time: 3 minutes

Ingredients:

¼ tsp Vanilla Extract

1 packet Gelatine, without sugar

1 tbsp. Heavy Whipping Cream

1/3 cup Boiling Water

2 tbsp. mashed Fruit

1 ½ cups crushed Ice

1/3 cup Cold Water

Preparation:

In the Power Pressure Cooker XL combine the gelatin and boiling water. Cook until dissolved on BEANS/LENTILS mode and with the lid off.

Transfer to a blender and add the remaining ingredients. Blend until smooth.

Serve immediately or freeze.

Nutrition information per serving:

Calories 173, Net Carbs 3.7 g, Fat 10 g, Protein 4 g

Raspberry and Coconut Cheesecake

Serves: 12

Prep + Cook time: 4 hours and 50 minutes

Ingredients:

2 Egg Whites

¼ cup Erythritol

3 cups desiccated Coconut

1 tsp Coconut Oil

¼ cup melted Butter

Filling:

3 tbsp. Lemon Juice

6 ounces Raspberries

2 cups Erythtitol

1 cup Whipped Cream

Zest of 1 Lemon

3 tbsp. Lemon Juice

24 ounces Cream Cheese

Preparation:

Apply the coconut oil to the bottom and sides Power Pressure cooker xl. Line with parchment paper. Set on CHICKEN/MEAT mode.

Mix all the crust ingredients and pour the crust into the pan. Cook for about 25 minutes. Let cool.

Meanwhile, beat the cream cheese until soft. Add the lemon juice, zest, and sweetener. In a mixing bowl, beat the heavy cream with an electric mixer. Fold the whipped cream into the cheese cream mixture. Fold in the raspberries gently. Spoon the filling into the baked and cooled crust. Place in the fridge for 4 hours.

Nutrition information per serving:

Calories 318, Net Carbs 4 g, Fat 31 g, Protein 5 g

Pecan Cookies

Serves: 12

Prep + Cook time: 25 minutes

Ingredients:

1 Egg

2 cups ground Pecans

¼ cup Sweetener

½ tsp Baking Soda

1 tbsp. Butter

20 Pecan Halves

Preparation:

Mix the ingredients, except the pecan halves, until combined. Make 20 balls out of the mixture and press them with your thumb onto a lined cookie sheet. Add them to the Power Pressure cooker xl. Set it on CHICKEN/MEAT mode. Top each cookie with a pecan half. Cook for about 12 minutes.

Nutrition information per serving:

Calories 101, Net Carbs 0.6 g, Fat 11 g, Protein 1.6 g

Keto Snickerdoodles

Serves: 16

Prep + Cook time: 25 minutes

Ingredients:

2 cups Almond Flour

½ tsp Baking Soda

¾ cup Sweetener

½ cup Butter, softened

Pinch of Salt

Coating:

2 tbsp. Erythritol Sweetener

1 tsp Cinnamon

Preparation:

Combine all the cookie ingredients in a bowl.

Make 16 balls out of the mixture. Flatten them with your hands. Combine the cinnamon and erythrol.

Dip the cookies in the cinnamon mixture and arrange them on a lined cookie sheet inside the Power Pressure Cooker XL. Cook for 15 minutes on CHICKEN/ MEAT mode.Perform a quick release and serve.

Nutrition information per serving:

Calories 131, Net Carbs 1.5 g, Fat 13 g, Protein 3 g

Chef's Selection Recipes

Hot Chicken Wings

Serves: 3

Prep + Cook time: 50 minutes

Ingredients:

2 tbsp Oil

6 Chicken Wings

4 cups Chicken Broth

¼ cup Cayenne Hot Pepper Sauce

4 tbsp Butter

2 tbsp Worcestershire Sauce

1 tsp Tabasco

Preparation:

Grease the stainless-steel insert with some oil and place the chicken wings. Pour in the chicken broth and cayenne hot pepper sauce. Seal the lid. Set the steam release handle and press the CHICKEN/MEAT button.

When you hear the cooker's end signal, perform a quick release and open the lid. Remove the wings from the broth and set aside.

In a large, non-stick skillet, melt the butter over medium-high heat. Add the wings and brown for 3-4 minutes, turning once. Finally, add the Worcestershire sauce and Tabasco. Give it a good stir and remove from the heat.

Nutrition information per serving:

Calories: 475, Protein: 24.9g, Carbs: 3.2g, Fats: 39.5g

Roast Beef with Béarnaise Sauce

Serves: 6

Prep + Cook time: 55 minutes

Ingredients:

2 lb. Beef Scotch Filet

3 tbsp Oil

4 tbsp Butter

1 cup White Wine

1 large Onion, finely chopped

1 tsp fresh Basil, finely chopped

4 Egg Yolks

2 cups Beef Broth

2 tbsp Lemon juice

5 Peppercorns

Preparation:

Melt butter on BEANS/LENTILS settings. Add onions and stir-fry until translucent. Add wine, basil, peppercorn, and lemon juice. Stir well and seal the lid. Set the steam release handle and cook for 5 minutes.

After you hear the cooker's end signal, perform a quick pressure release and open the lid. Stir in egg yolks and add beef filets. Pour in 2 cups of beef broth and close the lid. Set the steam release handle again and press the CHICKEN/MEAT button. Cook for 25 minutes. Serve warm with the sauce.

Nutrition information per serving:

Calories: 523, Protein: 48.2g, Carbs: 4g, Fats: 30.8g

Creamy Cauliflower Beef Stew

Serves: 4

Prep + Cook time: 20 minutes

Ingredients:

1 lb. Beef Stew Meat

1 cup of Cauliflower, chopped

1 medium Onion, sliced

2 cups Beef Broth

2 cups Heavy Cream

1 tsp Italian Seasoning mix

1 tsp Salt

½ tsp Chili Pepper, ground

Preparation:

Combine all ingredients in the pressure cooker. Close the lid and set the steam release handle. Press CHICKEN/MEAT button and cook for 15 minutes.

When done, press CANCEL and turn off the cooker. Perform a quick release to release the steam.

Nutrition information per serving:

Calories: 324, Protein: 25.9g, Carbs: 4.2g, Fats: 20g

Barbecue Wings

Serves: 4

Prep + Cook time: 15 minutes

Ingredients:

12 Chicken Wings

¼ cup Barbecue Sauce

1 cup of Water

Preparation:

Place the chicken wings and water in your Power Pressure Cooker XL. Close the lid and cook for 5 minutes on CHICKEN/MEAT setting. Release the pressure quickly.

Rinse under cold water and pat the wings dry. Place them in your Power Pressure Cooker and pour the barbecue sauce over. Mix with your hands to coat them well.

Select BEANS/LENTILS mode, close the lid and with the lid off, cook on all sides, until sticky.

Nutrition information per serving:

Calories 140.7, Carbohydrates 2 g, Fiber 0.2 g, Fat 3.3 g, Protein 19.5 g.

Asparagus Dressed in Bacon

Serves: 4

Prep + Cook time: 17 minutes

Ingredients:

1 pound of Asparagus

8 ounces of Bacon

1 cup of Water

Preparation:

Pour the water into your pressure cooker. Cut off the ends of the asparagus.

Slice the bacon in enough strips to cover each asparagus spear. Wrap the asparagus in bacon.

Arrange the wrapped asparagus on a steamer basket. Place the basket inside the Power Pressure Cooker. Close the lid and cook for 4 minutes on CHICKEN/MEAT.

Release the pressure quickly.

Nutrition information per serving:

Calories 224.4, Carbohydrates 5.8 g, Fiber 0.1 g, Fat 14.6 g, Protein 15.6 g

Pressure Cooked Deviled Eggs

Serves: 4

Prep + Cook time: 20 minutes

Ingredients:

4 Eggs

1 tsp Paprika

1 tbsp light Mayonnaise

1 tsp Dijon Mustard

1 cup of Water

Preparation:

Place the eggs and water in your Power Pressure Cooker XL. Close the lid and cook for 5 minutes on RICE/RISOTTO mode. Let the pressure release naturally.

Place the eggs in an ice bath and let cool for 5 minutes. Peel and cut them in half. Whisk together the remaining ingredients.

Top the egg halves with the mixture.

Nutrition information per serving:

Calories 100, Carbohydrates 0.7 g, Fiber 0.2 g, Fat 7.9 g, Protein 6.4 g

Pepper Meat

Serves: 6

Prep + Cook time: 50 minutes

Ingredients:

2 lb. of Beef Filet or another tender cut

4 Onions, peeled and finely chopped

2 cups of Water

1 tbsp of Tomato Paste

2 tbsp of Oil

1 tbsp of Butter, melted

2 tbsp of fresh Parsley, finely chopped

½ tsp of freshly Ground Black Pepper

Preparation:

Cut into bite-sized pieces and set aside. Grease the bottom of pressure cooker with oil.

Make the first layer with meat chops in your stainless-steel insert. Add finely chopped onions, tomato paste, fresh parsley, salt, and pepper. Give it a good stir and add about 2 cups of water.

Close the lid and set the steam release. Press the CHICKEN/MEAT button and cook for 30 minutes. Press CANCEL button and turn off the cooker. Release the steam naturally.

When done (the meat should be fork tender), stir in 1 tbsp melted butter.

Nutrition information per serving:

Calories: 382, Protein: 47.3g, Carbs: 4.3g, Fats: 16g

Conclusion

Thank you so much for purchasing this book. I have put a lot of hard work into making this a great resource for both experienced and beginner cooks, and I hope you get an immense amount of value out of the book.

I know not everyone likes to write book reviews, but would you mind taking a minute to write a review on Amazon? Even a short review works, and it would mean a lot to me and will help me improve and provide a better-quality product.

If someone you care about is struggling with anxiety or workaholism, please send him or her a copy of this book.

Made in the USA
Columbia, SC
06 January 2019